Prayer, Faith, Trials and Victory

Lessons of Faith and Perseverance for Victorious Christian Living

By Dale A. Robbins, D.Min.

Victorious Publications
Grass Valley, California – Nashville, Tennessee
www.victorious.org

Prayer, Faith, Trials and Victory

Copyright © 1995, 2015, Dale A. Robbins
Published by Victorious Publications
Grass Valley, California – Nashville, Tennessee
www.victorious.org

ISBN: 0964802236
ISBN-13: 978-0964802230

CONTENTS

INTRODUCTION

Prayer, Faith, Trials and Victory is a selection of inspiring testimonies, articles and Bible studies I've shared with audiences and readers in recent years regarding prayer and faith.

Of special personal significance to me, are the first and last chapters, which describe how I became a follower of Jesus, as well as the impact that my mother's prayers had on my life.

I was only 12-yrs-old when the Lord honored her prayers to spare the lives of our family during a deadly F-3 tornado. Then nearly ten years later, her prayers prevailed again for me... this time, for a wayward prodigal son, whom Christ eventually saved and called into the ministry.

Perhaps my testimony will help remind parents that their prayers for family and kids can be powerful and effective... and that the greatest faith is often found in the most common, humble people.

The remaining chapters provide many other helpful lessons and first-hand experiences, that I believe will strengthen your faith and bring glory and honor to our Lord and Savior.

May God use these words to encourage your prayer life, and to deepen your faith and relationship with Him!

Dale A. Robbins
Nashville, Tennessee

— 1 —
A Miracle in the Eye of the Storm
How God Heard My Mother's Prayers and Saved Our Lives in a Deadly Tornado

Spring in rural Indiana is a time of seasonal transition, from the cold ambience of winter, to warm, humid days interspersed with welcome rainstorms. It was only a week before Easter. Already the grass was green, flowers were budding, and the dogwood in the front yard had bloomed.

Sitting in church on Palm Sunday morning, it was hard to remain undistracted from the sounds of other kids playing outside in the unusually warm temperatures. Besides, I couldn't wait to get home and out of the starchy clothes... relatives were coming over for Sunday dinner.

Though sunny and hot, it was a relaxing afternoon under the shade trees sipping on lemonade with family. As dusk approached, the familiar sight of dark clouds were accumulating in the west. Distant sparks of lightning could be seen on the horizon, meaning a typical Midwest storm was brewing.

The family had gone indoors and were watching TV when news of a tornado warning scrawled across the screen. Such warnings were not unusual and didn't generate much concern until the program was later interrupted by a urgent news bulletin. They reported that moments earlier, a twister had devastated a community 15 miles to our west, and was headed due east, directly in our path. My parents became alarmed and realized it was time to take refuge in the basement.

My dad was the last of us to arrive below when the lights suddenly went out. We were fumbling to find a flashlight, when there was a hush. *"Do you hear that?"* Mother whispered. We stood motionless, straining to hear what seemed to be the increasing sound of a distant roar. But in mere seconds, the noise had become a rumbling vibration that was now shaking the structure above and around us.

Instinctively, we each knew the danger that was upon us, but there was no time to react. My heart was pounding in my chest. Behind me I could hear my mother's soft, familiar voice calling out to the Lord for His help. *"Dear Jesus, please help us!"*

Then suddenly we heard and felt the impact of a massive collision. The house shook violently. We were deafened by the sounds of breakage and the groanings of timbers being twisted and torn. Shocked by what was happening, we all peered out helplessly from the small basement window. In the dim light we could see a blurry collage of objects hurling past from the wind's great force... trees, farm machinery , huge objects. Near the window, a small tree bent completely to the ground without breaking.

Then as quickly as it had begun, there was silence. The tornado had apparently passed. We carefully emerged from the basement, and to our surprise, we found the house intact.

But when we pushed the front door open, the surrounding devastation was beyond belief. It appeared that a nuclear bomb had exploded. Fallen trees, portions of buildings, automobiles, clothing, home appliances... mangled debris of every kind covered the ground and hung from disfigured trees in all directions.

We had no injuries, but later we would discover the toll was more severe just a few miles up the road, where

The remains of a destroyed home and farm, whose owner and twelve others were killed in the Palm Sunday tornado that struck Sheridan, Indiana on April 11, 1965.

thirteen of our neighbors and friends were killed. Altogether, this and several other twisters in Indiana took the lives of 60 on the same day.

I knew that we were fortunate to be alive, but didn't realize the divine significance of this until later hearing the account of our neighbor from across the road. When he saw the funnel cloud coming, he quickly gathered his family in the car and raced away from its path. After reaching a safe distance away, he stopped and watched as the twister destroyed his home, then proceeded toward ours.

"I knew that if you were there, it would be all over for you," he said. *"But a strange thing happened. When the twister reached your driveway, I saw it lift up over your house and come down on the other side!"* As he said this, a tingle went up my spine! I realized this was same moment that my mother was praying, *"Dear Jesus, please help us!"*

This impacted my life in a dramatic way. Perhaps for the first time, I understood that prayer really works. Its power became a living reality to me, through the legacy of my mother's faith. Never would I forget this tremendous revelation, nor the miraculous answer to prayer which saved our lives on Palm Sunday, 1965.

Over the years, I've come to value the power of prayer more and more. Each day, as well as in times of crisis and distress, I've discovered that He is always there to strengthen and help His children, to respond to their pleas. And regardless of the size of problems that we may face – whether the fierce winds of a cyclone or the daily challenges of life, Jesus is there for you. Just call upon His name in faith and put your trust in Him.

"He shall call upon Me, and I will answer him; I will be with him in trouble; I will deliver him and honor him. 16 With long life I will satisfy him, And show him My salvation" (Psalms 91:15-16).

My mom and dad, Myron and Irene Robbins, standing in front of our farmhouse that had been in the path of the tornado. This photo was taken two years afterward.

5

— 2 —
The Victorious Christian Life
How to Rise Above Trials and Tragedy and Yet Remain Steadfast in Faith

"And this is the victory that has overcome the world–our faith." (1 John 5:4)

We all know what it is to have bad days and unfortunate moments in our life. However, few of us will ever have to face anything worse than the series of tragedies that occurred in the past to a Christian couple in Chicago... Horatio, age 43, and his wife, Anna, age 29.

Horatio was a successful businessman and church elder when an unexpected illness brought the death of his 4 year old little boy, Horatio Jr. And before he and Anna could even recover from the grief of this loss, another sudden tragedy occurred... a devastating fire that destroyed Horatio's business and financial interests. The family literally lost everything they owned and had to start over.

Then less than two years later, while planning a trip abroad with his wife and four daughters, Horatio was delayed and he sent his family on ahead by ship... only to learn a short time later that the vessel collided with another in the Atlantic and sank. His wife was one of only twenty-seven, out of several hundred passengers who survived... while all four daughters were drowned.

I cannot imagine the devastating loss and grief that these parents endured over this short period. It's a sad and painful thing to even recount this true story and think of the unimaginable grief they bore.

However, despite this catastrophe, they both remained steadfast, clinging to their faith in God. As Horatio made the long ocean journey to meet his surviving wife, he sailed past the site of his daughters watery graves. As he did, his grief was overcome with a greater sense of peace and victory in his soul, and was inspired to pen the words to what became a famous hymn of the church. Below is the first stanza from Horatio Spafford's hymn in 1873:

It is Well with My Soul
When peace, like a river, attendeth my way,
When sorrows like sea billows roll;
Whatever my lot, Thou hast taught me to say,
It is well, it is well with my soul.

This grieving father was able to attest of a wellness in his soul, not because of the tragic circumstances, but from his greater abiding trust and confidence in God.

Victory Comes by Faith

This kind of "peace" and inner "wellness" refers to an inward disposition of faith, an attitude of victorious confidence that refuses to surrender one's will to what appears as total defeat. While all appears to be lost, yet we trust in the unseen plan and purpose of the omnipotent God, in whom we have trusted our lives. He is in control, He is God almighty... and through Him, we will eventually rise above every adversity.

"Victory" refers to that inner peace of God which surpasses all understanding *(Philippians 4:7)*. It's the joy of the Lord which is our strength *(Nehemiah 8:10)*. It is the that inner confidence that overcomes discouragement, doubt and unbelief. It is the assurance that God is in control, and as we love the Lord and live a life wholly consecrated to Him, we know all things and circumstances are somehow working together for a good outcome. ***"And we know that all things work together for good to those who love God, to those who are the called according to His purpose" (Romans 8:28).***

God wants all his children to live a victorious life, however, this is only possible through the walk of faith. Faith is that which enables us overcome all the trials, adversities and circumstances of his world *(1 John 5:4)*. A victorious life of faith no longer lives by feelings, emotions or circumstances. It is no longer manipulated by the emotions of discouragement or depression. As people of faith, we live and abide according to what the Word of God says, not by what the circumstances say. ***"We walk by faith and not by sight" (2 Corinthians 5:7).*** This walk of faith is what brings victory.

Faith Enables Us to Endure

The scriptures teach that every Christian will face many trials and disappointments in this life and He promises to deliver us from them all. *"Many are the afflictions of the righteous: but the LORD delivers him out of them all" (Psalms 34:19).*

However, we must understand, our deliverance and victory may not always mean the immediate alteration of our circumstances. God may not always choose, or be at liberty, to change some external circumstances immediately. Instead, He will change YOU internally so that you can "endure" the circumstances. This is what Paul meant when he said he could be "content" regardless of what state he found himself *(Philippians 4:11)*. Despite our circumstances, we can have victory and peace in our heart, with the patience to endure until He alters our situation.

The story is told of a Christian wife who pled continually to the Lord about her alcoholic husband. She could not bear the continual heartache and embarrassment. She urgently prayed that God would transform the man and heal her marriage. Of course, God also wanted to change her husband, but He will not force anyone to serve him.

So since other than his drinking, he was good to his wife and was a good provider, the wife learned to endure and be patient for God to deal with her husband's heart.

In this situation, her deliverance came inwardly as the Lord relieved her burden by giving her His peace in her heart. Today her husband has still not turned to the Lord... but while she still prays for him, her peace and joy is no longer postponed to a future time when he might change. She lives each day in victory, with God's peace and joy rooted firmly in her heart.

God Provides Refuge, a Way of Escape

Difficult circumstances will never be unusual for anyone who serves the Lord. Sometimes such situations will only be short-lived "trials" that the Lord allows for a season, until He changes our circumstances. In other instances, difficult circumstances may be prolonged, requiring long-term endurance. Regardless, God's peace is not something that has to be put-on-hold until such storms or tribulations diminish. Even in the most oppressive or troublesome moments of our life, He promises to be a haven of rest and peace. *"The Lord also will be a refuge for the oppressed, A refuge in times of trouble" (Psalms 9:9).*

God promised to make a way of "escape" in the midst of distress, enabling us to "bear" certain temptations or trials. *"No temptation has overtaken you except such as is common to man; but God is faithful, who will not allow you to be tempted beyond what you are able, but with the temptation will also make the way of escape, that you may be able to bear it" (1 Corinthians 10:13).*

That way of "escape" is the presence and peace of God which abides in us to give us victory in the midst of the conflict... peace in the middle of turmoil. The presence of God in our life enables us to "bear" certain hardships and difficulties. And notice that it says He will not allow you endure an ordeal beyond your ability. That's something to always remember.

Paul – a Man of Faith, Victory, and Trials

Perhaps there is no one who knew how to live the victorious life better than the Apostle Paul. He was a man of great faith and strength with God, but he endured circumstances that were almost unbelievable. He wrote of his ordeals in the ministry:

"...in labors more abundant, in stripes above measure, in prisons more frequently, in deaths often. From the Jews five times I received forty stripes minus one. Three times I was beaten with rods; once I was stoned; three times I was shipwrecked; a night and a day I have been in the deep; in journeys often, in perils of waters, in perils of robbers, in perils of my own countrymen, in perils of the Gentiles, in perils in the city, in perils in the wilderness, in perils in the sea, in perils among

false brethren; in weariness and toil, in sleeplessness often, in hunger and thirst, in fastings often, in cold and nakedness– besides the other things, what comes upon me daily: my deep concern for all the churches" (2 Corinthians 11:23-28).

Despite his tribulations, Paul didn't lose sight of his victory. He wrote, *"We are hard pressed on every side, yet not crushed; we are perplexed, but not in despair; persecuted, but not forsaken; struck down, but not destroyed" (2 Corinthians 4:8-9).*

Paul's life and ministry were filled with tremendous hardship, but his attitude remained confident and resisted defeat. *"...But thanks be to God, who gives us the victory through our Lord Jesus Christ" (1 Corinthians 15:57).*

You Can Live in Victory, Not in Defeat!

If you are facing trying situations, don't allow them to rob you of your victory! The Bible tells us that "God is our refuge and strength, A very present help in trouble" *(Psalms 46:1)*. You are not alone. Jesus has promised to never leave you nor forsake you *(Hebrews 12:13)*. Turn your attention to Him and His Word. Wait upon Him and He will strengthen you with His peace. *"You will keep him in perfect peace, Whose mind is stayed on You, Because he trusts in You" (Isaiah 26:3).*

By faith, release your cares, your concerns and worries to Him. Trust Him to work out the end result. He will either change your circumstance or will change you to deal with them! Take His rest and peace upon you, believing that He has taken the burden from you. *"Cast all your cares upon him because he cares for you" (1 Peter 5:7).*

Remember and follow the Apostle Paul's example. He knew adversity at its worst, but also knew that circumstances need never threaten the joy and victory of the believer.

Paul said, *"Who shall separate us from the love of Christ? Shall tribulation, or distress, or persecution, or famine, or nakedness, or peril, or sword? ...Yet in all these things we are more than conquerors through Him who loved us" (Romans 8:35,37).*

— 3 —
When All Else Fails it's Time to Pray

How God Provided Miraculous Provisions in Response to Our Fervent Prayers

It was late Friday afternoon on the campus of Syracuse University. As I walked down the street, Bible in hand, a brisk November breeze whisked fallen leaves down the sidewalk. The trees gently swayed against the partly cloudy, blue sky. By this hour most classes had dismissed for the day. The campus was nearly deserted as students were elsewhere preparing for their weekend. I felt it was time to call it a day, the conclusion of a fruitful week of ministry for my wife and I.

For nearly a year we had been involved with campus evangelism, traveling across the U.S. to dozens of colleges to conduct street witnessing and evangelistic meetings. Married less than two years, these were adventurous times of faith for us. We had forfeited stable jobs and an apartment to answer God's calling. Now we made our home in a humble 8 x 14 foot travel trailer and relied solely on the Lord for our financial needs, which He always met... sometimes through the invitation to conduct a local church service, or perhaps from an unsolicited donation sent from friends or family.

In Syracuse, however, this pattern changed. For some

reason, God's provision had not come and our finances had dwindled to almost nothing.

That evening as we arrived back at our trailer parked in an empty lot, I tried to keep my panic to myself, but Jerri could see the worry on my face. Up to so faithful to provide. But there were only three dollars left in my wallet, one can of soup in the

Dale & Jerri Robbins, Age 22

cupboard, and we were more than a thousand miles away from family and friends. I felt like my back was against the wall. I had no idea what we would do.

After our meager supper, I sat near the window, quietly leafing through my Bible in the dim light. Tears streamed from my eyes. I began to wonder whether we were really called by God into this ministry. I felt discouraged, like giving up... but then I experienced a profound thought. Give up for what else? What alternative do I have? Who else but God do I have to turn to?

Just then my eyes fell upon a scripture passage, one that I had often preached from. ***"The effective, fervent prayer***

15

of a righteous man avails much" (James 5:16). As I pondered its meaning, I was reminded that the phrase "effective fervent" was translated from a single Greek word, *energeo (ἐνεργέω)*, a cousin to our word for energy. It can mean to "energize," similar to an electrical current that brings energy to a circuit. It suggests a prayer that is heartfelt, heated, passionate, enthusiastic, powerful, and persistent.

To me, effectual fervent prayer means to "pray like one's life depends on it." It is doggedly-persistent, faith-filled, whole-hearted and aggressive. And as I sat there dwelling on these thoughts, it appeared this was what the Lord wanted me to remember. It wasn't time for us to get discouraged or to give up. It was just time to pray... effectually and fervently.

Encouraged, yet still struggling with concern, Jerri and I spent the evening reminding ourselves of other encouraging scriptures. We read from many passages, such as when David wrote that he never saw the righteous forsaken or begging bread *(Psalms 37:25),* and when the Apostle Paul wrote that God promised to meet all our needs *(Philippians 4:19).*

Finally, having encouraged our faith as much as possible, we knelt at opposite ends of the little trailer to seek the Lord with all our heart. Though we had no idea what tomorrow would bring, we were determined to pray with the tenacity of Jacob, who wrestled persistently with the Angel until he received his blessing *(Genesis 32:24-28)*. Thus, into the late hours of the night we attempted to pray effectively and fervently, until sleep finally overtook us.

The next thing I remember is being awakened by an abrupt pounding at the trailer door. Groggily, I rubbed my eyes. From the window I could see the brilliant, orange sunrise behind the city skyline. A fresh, white blanket of snow now covered the ground. Again the knocking came.

I made my way to the door with some apprehension. We knew no one there, nor had any idea who this could be. *"Who is it,"* I said meekly. The mystery voice replied, *"I've got something for you."* Cautiously, I opened the door and there stood a short man with a funny sort of grin on his face and two brown grocery bags in his arms. To my surprise, he quickly shoved the bags in the doorway, then turned and pranced off through the snow without saying a word.

By this time Jerri had joined me. Neither of us were sufficiently awake to fully assess what was going on. Still stunned, we sat down and began to look through the bags. To our amazement there was bread, meat, canned goods and soups. Not just any variety, but several cans of my favorite soup. Ironically, these all were the same items and brands we normally purchased.

There was also a can of shaving cream... the same brand that I always buy. Who knew that I had just used my last ounce of shave cream the previous day? No razor blades were in the bag. Who could know that I still had an over-abundant supply of blades?

And finally in the bottom of one sack, there was an envelope of cash, which I discovered to be the amount needed to fill our gas tank, that took us to our next destination.

On that wintry, Saturday morning in Syracuse, my wife and I wept in the doorway of our trailer, giving thanks to God for hearing and answering our prayer. No one in Syracuse, nor on this planet, knew anything about our need, except our Lord God almighty. And it was He who dispatched the little, grinning man, perhaps an angel, to minister to us in our hour of need.

For many years, this experience has inspired our hearts and served as a precedent for many years of faith. We have come to trust the faithfulness of our Lord Jesus to answer the earnest prayers and meet the needs of His followers.

Indeed, when all else fails you, don't ever be discouraged or give up. **It's time to pray... effectually and fervently!**

— 4 —
Principles of Great Faith
A Closer Look at the Subject of Faith and How to Develop a More Effective Prayer Life

Matthew 8:5 "Now when Jesus had entered Capernaum, a centurion came to Him, pleading with Him, 8:6 saying, Lord, my servant is lying at home paralyzed, dreadfully tormented.
8:7 And Jesus said to him, I will come and heal him.
8:8 The centurion answered and said, Lord, I am not worthy that You should come under my roof. But only speak a word, and my servant will be healed.
8:9 For I also am a man under authority, having soldiers under me. And I say to this one, Go, and he goes; and to another, Come, and he comes; and to my servant, Do this, and he does it.
8:10 When Jesus heard it, He marveled, and said to those who followed, Assuredly, I say to you, I have not found such great faith, not even in Israel!"

The story of the believing centurion is probably the best illustration of great faith in the New Testament. Jesus was so impressed with the centurion, he remarked that he had not found such great faith in Israel – the entire Jewish nation.

One might think that such faith should have emerged

from one of the religious leaders of the day, such as the Scribes or Pharisees, most of whom had been students of the scriptures from their early youth. But this man was not even a Jew, but a gentile. To make matters more unique, he was a soldier in the Roman army, whose military occupation of Palestine was viewed with disdain by most Jews.

Ironic as it may seem, it isn't always the religious leaders, ministers, or theologians who aspire toward spiritual things. Often, it is the unsuspecting layman, the housewife, the farmer, the soldier or other humble, common people who demonstrate great faith in God. We must never lose sight that the Gospel is a simple message which has no respect of persons, nor requires any special credentials to believe it.

The legacy of the centurion is recorded without benefit of his name, but the title of his rank tells us that he was an officer with authority over 100 men. He was probably already a believer when he approached Jesus, seeing that he expressed such unusual comprehension of Christ's authority and identity *(Matthew 8:8-9)*.

Note that at no time did the centurion actually ask Jesus to heal the servant. He came to the Lord with a somber report of his servant's suffering, but stopped short of making any request for healing. Apparently he was trying to assess the Lord's will in the matter, awaiting his response to the crisis at hand. Perhaps he was hesitant of how Jesus would respond to the request of a non-Jew, especially since he was a soldier in the unpopular Roman army. Or maybe he wondered whether Jesus would even consider taking the time to help a mere servant.

Without hesitation, Jesus voluntarily offered to the centurion, *"I will come and heal him" (Matthew 8:7).* There was no more question whether it was the Lord's will to heal the servant. Not only was Jesus willing, but by his own suggestion, was ready to go out of his way to the centurion's home to perform the healing. What encouragement this must have been, to sense Jesus' compassion, to witness His eagerness to bring relief and healing to a poor sick soul of low estate.

The centurion's humble, confident response to all this was most remarkable. In essence he said, *"Lord, I'm unworthy to have you as a guest in my home, but because I am a man with authority and am acquainted with giving orders to others, I understand your authority, and know that all you have to do is speak your word and my servant will be healed" (Matthew 8:5-10).*

From the story of the centurion, there are four important principles which we learn about great faith:

(1) Great faith begins as a follower of Christ, knowing him personally, realizing his divine authority.

It is obvious that the centurion came to Jesus with an unusual perception of Christ's position and authority. It is likely that he had been an observer and a follower of Jesus for some time. This indicates that the first step toward a faith which results in answered prayers, is to be a follower of Jesus Christ.

We must have a proper relationship with Him, which enables us to approach God with the confidence that our heart is surrendered to the purpose of his will. Not only as our savior, but as Lord, our beloved master, whom we follow and serve with all our heart, endeavoring to keep his commandments and do those things which are pleasing to him. As the scripture says, ***"Beloved, if our heart does not condemn us, we have confidence toward God. And whatever we ask we receive from Him, because we keep His commandments and do those things that are pleasing in His sight" (1 John 3:21-22).***

(2) The motives of great faith are pure, and are in harmony with the will of God.

The centurion boldly brought his need to Jesus to find out what his will was concerning the afflicted servant. He was not presumptuous or demanding, but reverent and submissive. As for his motive, his concern was not for himself, but over the suffering and need of someone else – in fact, a mere servant of whom were often considered the lowest class of people.

It is necessary that we ascertain the will of God in respect to our desires and requests. The scriptures clearly indicate that God answers those prayers which are in accordance to His will, not just our own. To have faith's assurance for the desired results of our prayers, our requests must be based upon the criteria of God's wants and desires.

Prayer should not be viewed as merely a way to obtain our wishes, but a means that God uses to perpetrate His own desires. The Bible says, ***"Now this is the confidence that we have in Him, that if we ask anything according to His will, He hears us. And if we know that He hears us, whatever we ask, we know that we have the petitions that we have asked of Him" (1 John 5:14-15).***

God's will is revealed through the record of His Word to us, in the Bible. We can possess faith for anything promised to us in God's Word, and if we want God's provisions, it is necessary for us to bring our needs to Him. James said that we ***"do not have because we do not ask" (James 4:2).***

But he also warned that some prayers will go unanswered because of improper motives: ***"You ask and do not*** *receive, because you ask amiss, that you may spend it on your pleasures" (James 4:3).*

This refers to carnal, self-willed, evil desires of the flesh, and one of the major reasons for ineffectual prayer. Are most of our requests based upon our own selfish interests? Materialistic wants? Or, is our faith directed toward winning lost souls to Christ, praying for the sick and afflicted, or the needs of the poor and homeless? Our motives, in relationship with God's will, must be a major consideration in our faith.

(3) Great faith has a humble heart, cognizant of the grace and compassion of God, whereby He loves and blesses us.

There was no doubt of the sincere humility of the centurion and his apparent high esteem and honor, placed in the person of Jesus. He confessed his unworthiness, his lowly undeserving status for Jesus to even come into his home.

The scripture states that *"God resists the proud, but gives grace to the humble" (James 4:6).* The word "humble" means self-abasement. We are totally dependent upon God, His mercy and His strength. What God does for us, in response to our requests, is not because we have earned or deserve anything. What God does is because of His love and grace (unmerited favor) manifested through the redemption of Jesus Christ. He tells us that when we

24

are in need, to come unto the throne of His "grace," that we might find His help. The Bible says, ***"Let us therefore come boldly to the throne of grace, that we may obtain mercy and find grace to help in time of need" (Hebrews 4:16).***

(4) Great faith has a complete trust in the dependability of God's Word, and accepts it as fact above any other evidence or circumstance.

The centurion was so thoroughly convinced of the authority of Christ's Word that He did not find it necessary for Jesus to personally visit the servant. He felt assured that if Christ would only just give the command, the healing would respond. He did not need to see anything or feel anything, but was willing to rest solely upon the premise of the spoken Word.

Such were the characteristics of Abraham's faith, who believed God's Word of promise, even though all natural circumstances were against him and there were no signs of the promise for seventeen years. ***"He did not waver at the promise of God through unbelief, but was strengthened in faith, giving glory to God, and being fully convinced that what He had promised He was also able to perform" (Rom. 4:20-21).***

God's Word is the very basis of our faith. His Word is the source of all creation, and nothing can withstand its power or force. His Word is absolutely trustworthy, in fact more trustworthy than the things of this world, that we can see or perceive with our senses. The believer must surrender his total confidence to the Word, even without any shred of visible evidence, or even in spite of contrary evidence.

In conclusion, the legacy of the believing centurion serves as a constant reminder that God is no respecter of persons, and that He will honor the faith of anyone who will dare to take Him at His Word.

"And it is impossible to please God without faith. Anyone who wants to come to him must believe that God exists and that he rewards those who sincerely seek him." (Hebrews 11:6 NLT)

Prayer Changed America's History, and Can Do it Again!

Despite America's Spiritual Decline, History Offers Hope For Another Spiritual Awakening

Today we face what seems to be a hopeless condition in America. Gross immorality has engulfed the land. Crime has taken over the streets. Sexual promiscuity and perversion fills our society. Drunkenness and drug abuse is everywhere. God has been rejected by most of our citizens... virtually kicked out of our government and our schools.

A few years ago, the legendary evangelist, Billy Graham, issued a profound warning, that *"If God doesn't soon bring judgment upon America, He'll have to go back and apologize to Sodom and Gomorrah!"*

How far it seems that the United States has drifted from its rich religious heritage. But many may not realize, that despite our nation's Christian beginnings, after only a few short years of its founding, it had already declined to a level of moral decadence and depravity that would rival today's sad condition.

According to the late church historian, J. Edwin Orr,[1] during the post-Revolutionary War years, drunkenness was of epidemic proportions. Of a population of four million, three hundred thousand were considered drunkards. Bank robberies occurred daily. Street crime, rape and murder was rampant and citizens were afraid to go out of their homes at night. Profanity was the worst imaginable, shocking in its filthiness.

The spiritual climate of the nation was disparaging. The Presbyterians met in general assembly to deplore the ungodliness of the country. Both the Methodists and Baptists were losing more members than they were gaining. The Lutherans and Episcopalians were struggling, and even considered a merger for the sake of survival.

Episcopal Bishop of New York, Samuel Provoost, had confirmed no one for so long that he quit the ministry. Samuel Shepherd, a pastor in Lenox, Massachusetts, said that he had not taken one young person into church membership in sixteen years.

A poll at Harvard revealed that there was not one believer in the entire student body. At Princeton, only two believers were discovered among the students, and Christianity was generally ridiculed. A mock communion was conducted at Williams College, and anti-Christian plays were performed at Dartmouth.

In New Jersey, a Bible was taken from a Presbyterian church and burned in a public bonfire. Christians were such a minority on campuses that they met in secret and kept minutes in code so they wouldn't be caught or persecuted.

The Chief Justice of the United States, John Marshall, wrote that the Church was *"too far gone ever to be revived."* Kenneth Scott Latourette, the Church historian, said, *"It looked as though Christianity were a waning influence, about to be ushered out of the affairs of men."*

Indeed, it appeared that the church in America was an endangered species. By all indications, the nation had rejected the Christianity of their forefathers. Sin and moral decay flourished.

But then something incredible occurred that changed what seemed to be an impossible situation. A revival of prayer erupted... one that changed the destiny of our nation!

The awakening of prayer seemed to first begin in the British Isles. In 1792, just a year after the death of John Wesley, a renewed spiritual hunger and revival began to take hold in Great Britain. John Erskine, a minister in Edinburgh, Scotland, wrote a little book on prayer which stirred the hearts of people, and sent a copy to the famed New England theologian, Jonathan Edwards. He along with another New England preacher, Baptist Pastor Isaac Backus, were instrumental in arousing a national interest to pray.

In 1794, the spiritual climate in America was at its worst when Backus called upon the ministers of every American church to unite in prayer for the nation. God was with these efforts, and churches of every denomination responded to the national appeal. Soon, a network of prayer meetings emerged across the country, coordinated to pray in unison, beginning on the first Tuesday of January, 1795, and once each quarter thereafter.

Predictably, as people sought God, signs of revival began to be seen. It was first evident in New England, sweeping through Connecticut then on to Massachusetts.

In Logan County Kentucky, where sin was somewhere on the scale of Sodom and Gomorrah, a Presbyterian minister, James McGready, held unified prayer meetings every third Saturday and at sunrise on Sundays. In a letter, he wrote that most of the winter of 1799, was spent weeping and mourning with the people of God.

Finally in the summer of 1800, great camp meeting revivals swept Kentucky and Tennessee, then burst over into North and South Carolina and swept the frontier.

Some years ago, I visited Cane Ridge, Kentucky where one of these great camp meetings converged for six days in August of 1801. It was here that the Christian Church denomination, as well as other fellowships, marked their origin. The historical placards described how over twenty thousand persons, from all over the country, came together almost intuitively, without any promotion or organized campaign.

At night, the hills and fields of the sparsely populated Bourbon County glimmered with torches as far as the eye could see, as smaller cells of hundreds gathered simultaneously around bonfires to hear rousing sermons by any one of dozens of preachers until the late hours.

Spiritual fervor was intense. The distant sounds of revival were heard in every direction from the bonfire gatherings. The hollows and ridges echoed with the barely audible, medley of preaching, repentant weeping and joyful praises.

These and other similar meetings and events became typical of the great American revival spawned through prayer. This remarkable widespread response to prayer restored America's spiritual soul and brought God's blessing for about a hundred years.

Yes, today America looks hopeless. It appears morally and spiritually bankrupt. But as we have discovered, there is always hope if God's people will come together and pray. God has salvaged our nation before, and can do it again. As Matthew Henry once wrote, *"When God intends great mercy for his people, he first of all sets them praying."*

Let's not give up on America, but let us embrace God's great promise of prayer. As His Word says:

"If my people, which are called by my name, shall humble themselves, and pray, and seek my face, and turn from their wicked ways; then will I hear from heaven, and will forgive their sin, and will heal their land" (2 Chronicles. 7:14).

---

[1] *Prayer and Revival, by J. Edwin Orr, 1912-1987*

— 6 —
Extraordinary Prayer By Ordinary People
God Answers the Prayers of Common People, Not Just Spiritual Giants

"Ask, and it will be given to you; seek, and you will find; knock, and it will be opened to you." (Matthew 7:7)

Most Christians have heard these simple words of Jesus many times before from Matthew 7:7. However, despite common familiarly with such verses, it's not likely that the Lord's promise to answer prayer will ever be taken for granted by Mrs. Cindy Hartman. This pastor's wife from Conway, Arkansas experienced a divine intervention that would even arouse the faith of many skeptics.

In July of 1994, Cindy was confronted in her home by a pistol-wielding burglar. The unknown man who surprised her when she came in to answer the phone, ripped the cord from the wall and ordered her into a closet. She was obviously fearful for her life, but didn't panic.

To the shock of the gunman, Cindy immediately fell to her knees and began to pray for God's Help. He was even more stunned when she boldly asked if she could pray for him! She proceeded to tell him about Christ's love and expressed her forgiveness for his actions.

Apparently this was more than the robber bargained for, and he began to weep as he knelt and prayed with her. To her relief, the man then yelled out the window to a woman waiting in a pickup: *"We've got to unload all of this stuff. This is a Christian home and we can't do this to them."* While the thieves returned her furniture, Cindy remained on her knees praying. Then the man used a shirt to wipe off his fingerprints, apologized and departed, even leaving his gun behind!

This amazing story, reported nationally by Associated Press,[1] is especially inspiring as it shows how willing God is to intervene in the behalf of His children when asked. The Bible says, ***"Let us therefore come boldly to the throne of grace, that we may obtain mercy and find grace to help in time of need" (Hebrews 4:16).***

Simply stated, there is no problem too big for God... and He invites any of His children to come and ask for His help. "Come boldly," he says... because He is full of "grace" and "mercy" to help us, in those things that trouble us.

Whether confronted by the impassible gulf of a Red Sea, as was the wandering Israelites, or bound by prison chains and stocks, as once were Paul and Silas... God's power to intervene and help, is just as potent in our modern times as He was in the era of New Testament. As scripture states, *"Jesus Christ is the same yesterday, today, and forever" (Hebrews 13:8).*

And perhaps most amazing of all, is that what God will do for one, He will do for any of us who will believe. He doesn't care about our social status, or how important or unimportant we might be. The Lord is no respecter of persons (*Acts 10:34*), and He will honor the prayers of servants as faithfully as He will for Kings. He will attend to the prayers of a common housewife, as much as He will for a noted theologian or famous preacher (*1 Peter 1:17*).

And although we often share a larger-than-life view of the famous Bible heroes who prayed and experienced remarkable miracles, the scriptures make it clear that these were just ordinary people like ourselves. *"Elijah was a man with a nature like ours, and he prayed earnestly..." (James 5:17-18).*

God will hear and answer the sincere, faith-filled prayer of "anyone" who is right with Him. *"The effective, fervent prayer of a righteous man avails much" (James 5:16).*

So it is, whenever you find yourself in need, or immersed in perplexity or crisis, boldly knock on heaven's door and call upon the Lord in faith. He cares about your every need and concern, and is eager to hear your prayer... to bring His help and blessing!

"Because he loves me, says the LORD, I will rescue him; I will protect him, for he acknowledges my name. He will call upon me, and I will answer him; I will be with him in trouble, I will deliver him and honor him. With long life will I satisfy him and show him my salvation" (Psa. 91:14-16).

[1] *Associated Press, July 29, 1994*

— 7 —
In God We Trust
Americans Need to Put Their Hope in God, Not Politicians or the Government

"It is better to trust in the Lord Than to put confidence in man." (Psalms 118:8)

The phrase first appeared on a two-cent coin in 1864, during the fervor of the Civil War. The bloody conflict had driven masses of Americans to their knees, and such sentiments of trust in God were widespread. Nearly 100 years later, after surviving two world wars and numerous other national adversities, such sentiments of faith remained high, which led to an act of congress in 1956, making *"In God We Trust"* the official U.S. motto that still appears today on U.S. currency.

However, what a difference a hundred-fifty years makes. Long-gone are the days which most American families attended church on Sundays, and viewed prayer and faith in God as vital to their survival. Since those times, beginning especially in the 1960's, America began a prolonged spiritual decline that has affected every facet of our culture.

Over a span of 50 years, God and His influence has been largely dismissed from much of our society. Today, Biblical values and morals are generally rejected by our peers, and ridiculed by Hollywood and the entertainment industry. The public school system has effectively kicked God out of the nation's classrooms, and our government and leaders have become predominantly godless and corrupt.

"In God We Trust" doesn't seem to be an appropriate fit for today's America, steeped in narcissism, immorality and depravity. However, there's still a glimmer of encouraging news for the old relic. According to a 2003 Gallup Poll, at least 90% of Americans still approve of the inscription on U.S. coins.

What an irony, that while Americans tried so hard to forget God, to exclude Him or His influences... a reminder of trusting Him still remains as close as every pocket or purse. Obviously, the inscription didn't originate there by coincidence... but was an act of God, to drop His divine calling card in our pockets to remind us where to look for strength and encouragement.

So if Americans are still okay with the old motto, what does that mean? Maybe nothing, but then again it could imply that, while most still don't have much of an appetite for God or His ways, some may think that trusting in God might still be a future backup option if everything else fails. Or maybe it's a sign of dormant faith, that could yet reawaken under the right circumstances.

Considering the rising tide of problems and crises for our nation in recent times, it's possible that people might start looking to the Lord for their answers again. Many are deeply worried and confused about what's happening across our land... fearful about the future, the rising threat of terrorism, the unstable economy as well as the uncertainty of political leadership.

Maybe this would be a good time for everyone to take out a coin and review the meaning of that old inscription again. While society long-ago redirected their dependence away from God, and toward man and his institutions instead... some might start to realize man's limitations and the need to look to God's help again.

Perhaps this need will be most easily seen in the futility of our chaotic political system. As our nation became more sophisticated and godless, most stopped looking to the Lord for their answers, and started electing candidates to solve their problems. Such issues, however, can reach such levels of intensity and complexity, that man simply can't solve them.

Needless to say, America faces many challenges today that no elected politician can fix... and regardless of whether they realize it, they need God's help. That's where all Christians need to get involved.

First, as citizens, believers should vote in every election and participate in the political process. We should support, speak up for, and pray for political candidates who embrace our freedom-loving Christian values, and who oppose those politics and philosophies that seek to destroy the freedom and values of our nation.

But after we've exercised such rights, and have done all we can do, we must then trust God with what follows. More than all our physical labors, we need to go to knees and pray for those who have been elected. Regardless of whether they follow Christ or share our views, we must pray that God will influence His will and guidance in their decisions... for our sakes, as well as for our nation.

Many of us may look back at recent elections with disappointment. We prayed, sought God's wisdom to vote for candidates we believed would be honest, trustworthy and who could provide good leadership... and were dismayed to see that many other voters could not see things as clearly as we did. But we have to realize that even whenever we can manage to elect those who seem to be the right candidates, they are only human with mortal weaknesses, and can sometimes do more to displease than please us. We all can probably think of some we supported who failed our expectations... while occasionally others we opposed, surprised us by better-than-expected performance.

The fact is, regardless of "who" is elected to any political office... or whoever serves as the nation's president, we never know for sure what we will get. Politicians and leaders are mere mortals, so either way, regardless of who's elected, we still must "Trust God" and pray for His will to be done through them. We must pray that God can either help them remain true to the values and judgment we thought they had, or turn them around completely and bring them to their senses. God can also, of course, remove a leader when He sees it to be His will.

It was the Apostle Paul who encouraged the church to pray for secular leaders, including the "king" and "all those in authority" *(1 Timothy 2:1-3)*, while at the same time suffering great persecution and imprisonment at their hands. In fact, Nero, Rome's emperor at that time, was one of the most despicable persecutors of the church. Among other vile exploits against believers, it was said that he captured Christians, *"dipped them in oil, and then set them on fire in his garden at night as a source of light."*

According to Eusebius, a historian and bishop of Caesarea in the second century, both Peter and Paul were eventually killed at the orders of Nero, who ironically committed suicide later the same year that Paul was executed in 68 A.D.

Paul's admonishment just a couple years or so prior to this, takes on special significance, as he knew how important it was to pray for such leaders. Although he would be martyred by this wicked tyrant, Paul had trusted the Lord with his fate, knowing that his life was not at the mercy of the emperor, but was surrendered to the will and purposes of God.

Therefore, let us all be encouraged to realize that earthly leaders do not control our destiny, only God. Thus, let us put our trust in Him, rather than man.

"I urge you, first of all, to pray for all people. Ask God to help them; intercede on their behalf, and give thanks for them. Pray this way for kings and all who are in authority so that we can live peaceful and quiet lives marked by godliness and dignity. This is good and pleases God our Savior..." (1 Timothy 2:1-3 NLT).

— 8 —
Things May Be Better
Than You Think
Contentment With Life Doesn't Have to Be Postponed

"Not that I speak in regard to need, for I have learned in whatever state I am, to be content." (Philippians 4:11)

"Hi Pastor! Remember me?" I reached out to shake the visitor's hand, while performing a quick review of my memory banks, but it was no use. *"I hope you'll forgive me. I just can't place you,"* I said. With a big smile on his face, the gentleman replied, *"You haven't forgotten me already have you? I'm Martin!"*

Ah yes, it began to came back to me as I placed his name with his face. Martin had been a church member at one of my former pastorates. *"Why Martin... it's great to see you again! How are things with you?"* I said.

As Martin talked on, my recollection of the past grew stronger, but my enthusiasm began to wane as I remembered that my association with him had not always been all that pleasant. My recollection was that Martin was seldom happy with me or the church. He complained often, was a frequent dissenter at business meetings, and had even left and returned to the church on several occasions.

43

Predictably, his conversation soon took on a negative tone, but with a surprising twist. *"Things have never been the same at that church since you were there,"* he said. *"Those were the good ole' days!"*

Good ole' days? Did my ears deceive me, or was Martin describing his previous unhappy years at our church as good ole' days? I was amazed and somewhat amused to hear him continue to compliment the church of the past, as he contrasted it with his miserable appraisal of the present church. The irony of it all was that his complaints were the same as they had always been, but he now somehow viewed the former as better than the present.

"How ironic!" I thought to myself. Many people will go through life disappointed, finding fault with everything, but will later look back with fondness, realizing that it was "better than what they thought." In reality, they're in the midst of the good ole' days, and don't even know it!

Many people struggle with what I call the "greener grass syndrome." To them, the grass is always greener on the other side of the fence. Their contentment with life is always attached to some other place, some other time, or with someone else. The solution to their marital problems is to get a new wife or husband. The answer to their dissatisfaction in the work place is to get a different job. They look at their circumstances as if they were a paper cup, to be crumpled and tossed in the trash in exchange for a new one.

Unfortunately, our modern "feel good" culture has helped to shape these attitudes that feed such carnal impulses. A society of painkillers, fast food, and technological marvels has taught us that anything that is less than perfect, instantaneous or self-gratifying should be aborted... like an unwanted unborn baby. In essence, we learn that problems are mere inconveniences that should be "avoided and discarded," instead of being accepted as "character-building challenges that should be overcome." Is it no wonder why it is rare to find anyone with genuine character today?

Contentment really has nothing to do with circumstances, but it has everything to do with one's attitude. Basically life is made up of about 10% of what happens to you, and 90% of how you react to it. For some people, problems represent barriers that end their progress... but to others, they represent hurdles to be leaped over. We may not be able to change the destiny of circumstances that we will face in life, but we can change our attitude toward them.

Believe it or not, regardless of how bad it may sometimes seem, things are never as bad as they could be. And wouldn't it be ironic that if someday, when persons face things that are even worse, they will reflect back on their present circumstances and think of them as the best times in their life! Some people are so obsessed with the thorns, that they don't realize that they're sitting in a rose bush.

Despite whatever challenges you face, don't postpone your happiness to some other time or place, and don't be blinded from the good things that God has placed around you today. An intimate relationship with Jesus Christ is the only thing that brings true inner contentment. So be filled with the love of Jesus, and smell the roses that God has put in your life. Lighten up... and enjoy the good ole' days!

"Finally, brethren, whatever things are true, whatever things are noble, whatever things are just, whatever things are pure, whatever things are lovely, whatever things are of good report, if there is any virtue and if there is anything praiseworthy; meditate on these things" (Philippians. 4:8).

— 9 —

The Most Common Reasons for Unanswered Prayers

*How to Become More Effective in Receiving
Answers to Prayer*

One of the greatest benefits afforded to every Christian is
the privilege of answered prayers. In the Bible, Jesus
made this tremendous promise, ***"And whatever things
you ask in prayer, believing, you will receive"
(Matthew 21:22).***

However, despite the Lord's willingness to answer prayer,
it is obvious that some prayers have gone unanswered.
Why is this? The following are some of the most common
reasons why some prayers do not get results:

1. Lack of Fellowship with God and His word

***John 15:7 "If you abide in Me, and My words abide
in you, you will ask what you desire, and it shall be
done for you."***

Unanswered prayers are sometimes a result of an absence
of fellowship with the Lord and His Word. Jesus promised
that if we would remain in His fellowship, and allow His
Word to remain in us, this would produce results in
prayer.

2. Not Seeking to Please the Lord

1 John 3:22 "And whatever we ask we receive from Him, because we keep His commandments and do those things that are pleasing in His sight."

Answers to prayer come when we seek to keep His commandments and please the Lord with our life. This is not to suggest that we "earn" answered prayers, any more than we can earn salvation which comes only by faith *(Ephesians 2:8-9)*. He answers our prayers from his "grace" and "mercy" *(Hebrews 4:16)*, not merely from our good deeds. However, keeping His commandments and pleasing the Lord is a product of our obedience to His word, which is faith in action *(James 2:20)*.

What are His commandments? He commanded that we are to love the Lord with all our heart, mind, and soul, and to love our neighbor as ourselves *(Mark 12:30-31)*. Further, Jesus said we are to love our brethren as He has loved us. *"This is My commandment, that you love one another as I have loved you" (John 15:12).* Lack of love, bitterness, unforgiveness is the root of many unanswered prayers, since faith works by love *(Galatians 5:6)*.

3. Unconfessed Sin in One's Life

1 Peter 3:12 "For the eyes of the LORD are on the righteous, And His ears are open to their prayers;

But the face of the LORD is against those who do evil."

There is no doubt that sin will disrupt the flow of God's blessings and answers to prayer. The psalmist, David wrote, *"If I regard iniquity in my heart, The Lord will not hear" (Psalms 66:18).* All acts of rebellion and disobedience to God is considered sin. Sins of "commission," are those overt acts which are done in disobedience. However, sins of "omission," are those things we don't do in obedience, but know we should *(James 4:17).* The remedy for all sin is to confess it to God, forsake it, and ask Him to forgive you *(1 John 1:9).*

4. Improper Motives

James 4:3 "You ask and do not receive, because you ask amiss, that you may spend it on your pleasures."

Our motives in our prayer requests are of concern to the Lord. He wishes to help us in our time of need, but is not obligated to answer prayers which will merely feed our carnal, worldly appetites and *(lustful)* pleasures. Our motives and desires can be corrected by humbling ourselves, and drawing near to God *(James 4:8-10).*

5. Not asking in God's will

1 John 5:14-15 "Now this is the confidence that we

have in Him, that if we ask anything according to His will, He hears us. And if we know that He hears us, whatever we ask, we know that we have the petitions that we have asked of Him."

God will only answer those prayers that are in "His" will. When we ask anything that is in His will, we can have assurance that those "petitions" (requests) are granted to us. God's will is revealed through His Word, the Bible. Anything promised by His Word is His will, and we can be confident that He'll honor our prayers based on His Word.

6. Don't Know How to Pray

Luke 11:1 "...Lord, teach us to pray..."

Some lack effectiveness in prayer simply because they don't know what the scriptures teach about prayer. Jesus gave His disciples an outline for prayer in Matthew 6:9-13. Take the time to study it. Other passages teach that prayer is primarily to be a private, intimate time with the Lord *(Matthew 6:6)*, to be intermingled with praise and thanksgiving *(Acts 16:25, Philippians 4:6)*. Times of fasting with prayer are beneficial to strengthen our faith and power in prayer *(Acts 14:23, 1 Corinthians 7:5)*. Jesus often went to secluded places to spend prolonged periods in prayer *(Luke 6:12, Matthew 4:2)*.

7. Lack of Faith

Hebrews 11:6 "But without faith it is impossible to please Him, for he who comes to God must believe that He is, and that He is a rewarder of those who diligently seek Him."

We cannot please God without faith. Prayer is not merely "begging" from God. It is "believing" God and His Word! Faith will come forth and grow as we devote our attention to the Word of God *(Romans 10:17)*. Our faith can also be "built up," by praying in the Holy Spirit *(Jude 1:20)*.

8. Misunderstanding of Faith

Mark 11:24 "Therefore I say to you, whatever things you ask when you pray, believe that you receive them, and you will have them."

Many do not understand that faith is believing in the reality of things, even though we cannot see them *(Hebrews 11:1)*. Jesus said that "when" you pray, you must believe that you "receive" your answer at that moment. The word, "receive" comes from the Greek word, *lambanō (λαμβάνω)*, which means "to receive now" (present tense). He then says we will "have" them. "Have" comes from, *esomai (ἔσομαι),* which means "to possess later" (future tense).

So, when we pray we must believe in the finished results of our prayer, and we will eventually experience the tangible results sometime later.

9. Wavering faith

James 1:6-7 "But let him ask in faith, with no doubting, for he who doubts is like a wave of the sea driven and tossed by the wind. For let not that man suppose that he will receive anything from the Lord;"

There are those who allow every "wind" of circumstances to influence or discourage their faith. They vacillate back and forth, like the waves tossed about in the sea. One day they believe, but the next, they're ready to give up, and so forth. Such persons usually base their faith on their feelings or emotions instead of God's Word. They who waver in their faith cannot expect to receive "anything of the Lord." Our faith must become stable, steadfast, and consistent to receive from God.

10. Failure to apply spiritual Authority

Mark 11:23 "For assuredly, I say to you, whoever says to this mountain, Be removed and be cast into the sea, and does not doubt in his heart, but believes that those things he says will be done, he will have whatever he says."

There are times that some prayers may not get far until we incorporate the spoken authority of the name of Jesus. The reason for this is that the problems we face may "sometimes" be a product of an evil spiritual origin. As Paul writes, ***"For we do not wrestle against flesh and blood, but against principalities, against powers, against the rulers of the darkness of this age, against spiritual hosts of wickedness in the heavenly places" (Ephesians 6:12).*** In such cases, our prayers may need to engage in what we call "spiritual warfare" to obtain results.

The need for this type of prayer is most obvious whenever Christians deal directly with demonic activity. For this evil operation to cease, our prayers need to include the exercise of spiritual authority against the devil in the name of Jesus, commanding him to leave *(Acts 16:18)*. Therefore, as Jesus indicated, there will be times that we may need to literally speak to mountains (symbolic of obstacles, problems or strongholds) and tell them to move in Jesus' name.

11. Lack of Perseverance

Galatians 6:9 "And let us not grow weary while doing good, for in due season we shall reap if we do not lose heart."

Probably the greatest reason that some prayers go unanswered is because many give-up praying and believing before they receive their answer. As long as we have the promise of God's Word, be patient and persistent. Keep believing, and don't quit, no matter how long it takes! God has a "due season" when He will bring the answer to pass.

Finally, while these truths will provide insight to the pitfalls to avoid that can hinder our prayers, there will still be those instances that none of us can explain. I regret that sometimes there will be unanswered prayers that seem to have no reason, except only to trust by faith that it simply wasn't the Lord's will for this present time.

In such times, don't falter or give up, but *"Trust in the Lord with all your heart, And lean not on your own understanding" (Proverbs 3:5).*

— 10 —
All Things Work Together for Good
Why Bad Things Happen, and How God Can Turn Them Around for Good

"And we know that all things work together for good to those who love God, to those who are the called according to His purpose" (Romans 8:28).

The phone rang sometime around 3:00 am. For a pastor it's not unusual to get a call at that hour, but it's rarely good news. *"My little boy is dying,"* said the frantic voice on the phone. *"I'm on my way to the emergency room now, please be in prayer and meet me there!"*

The distressed caller didn't give his name before hanging up, but I knew it was Ben, one of the members of our church. His little boy, Craig, had struggled with a rare medical defect from birth. Within a few minutes I was out the door, racing up the highway toward the medical center. Not only was I deeply concerned for his son, but also for Ben, whose faith had been tested deeply by recent misfortune in his life, especially the health of his child.

Arriving at the emergency room, I found Ben, who quickly alerted me that the doctor had ordered an immediate life-flight of his son to a larger, distant hospital. As Craig laid on the gurney, we barely had a moment to pray for him, then the crew rushed in moving him quickly down the hall toward the waiting chopper. Ben and I ran behind onto the flight deck... but I stopped short to allow him a few brief seconds alone with his little boy as they strapped him in for the flight.

Because of limited space and weight Ben was not allowed to fly along. Instead, we both would make the trip by car and meet them there. But before they closed the door to lift off, he reached out one last time to touch the hand of his child... amidst tears, calling his name, asking the Lord to save his baby boy. It was both a heart-wrenching and surreal scene to observe. The father was weeping, praying, kneeling on the tarmac... while the chopper throttled its engines, lights flashing, lifting slowly above the powerful gusts. His tear-stained cheeks continued to point up toward the rising craft, hands outreached and praying until it was out of sight.

I'll never forget the images of that night, which brought about at least two remarkable results. First, the Lord answered the prayers of many and little Craig eventually recovered and went on to a normal, healthy life. The second occurred with his father, Ben, whose life began a transformation that evening. During his moments of desperation and travail, clinging to his child's life, he reached out to God with all his heart... and God reached back, pulling this dad closer to Himself than ever before. It was a painful thing to watch a father's trauma and desperate cries... but this together with the coming weeks and months of his son's recovery, deepened his faith and changed his life dramatically.

This was the precise kind of situation the Apostle Paul was referring to when he told the Christians at Rome that *"all things work together for good to those who love God" (Romans 8:28).* For this young Christian father, it seemed like his entire world was collapsing around the crisis with son... but the Lord turned this harrowing circumstance around and literally caused everything to work together for good.

During my years as a pastor I have preached and taught from this passage in Romans 8:28 hundreds of times, but from my observations I'm convinced that for many it remains one of the least understood and appreciated passages of the Bible. It's tough for many to grab hold of the idea that God doesn't let anything go to waste in our lives, that He has a purpose and a reason for everything that happens in the lives of His followers, and will even use the bad and difficult things to produce good in our behalf.

We all know from experience that life will often bring many hardships, disappointments and heartaches. But for those who love Him and follow Him, God promises to make such things "work together" for good. That is, to serve a higher purpose, to bring about beneficial results.

The Amplified Bible, a translation which helps more fully illuminate the meanings and nuances from the original texts, puts it this way: ***"We are assured and know that [God being a partner in their labor] all things work together and are [fitting into a plan] for good to and for those who love God and are called according to [His] design and purpose" (Romans 8:28 TAB).***

Why Doesn't God Just Allow Good things to Happen?

Jesus and His disciples taught repeatedly that trials and tribulations were sure to come to all of God's people *(James 1:12, 2 Timothy 3:12)*, and were actually necessary to perfect the faith and spiritual character of God's people. James in fact wrote that such occurrences should be viewed not as something negative, but with joyful optimism... as opportunities for their faith to grow.

"Dear brothers and sisters, when troubles come your way, consider it an opportunity for great joy. For you know that when your faith is tested, your endurance has a chance to grow. So let it grow, for when your endurance is fully developed, you will be perfect and complete, needing nothing" (James 1:2-4 NLT).

Paul also taught that a believer's faith and character must be refined, purified, tempered in order to grow and reach greater levels of maturity for God... so He can make us into what He wants us to be, or to perform the work that He has called for us to do. He said, ***"We can rejoice, too, when we run into problems and trials, for we know that they help us develop endurance. And endurance develops strength of character, and character strengthens our confident hope of salvation" (Romans 5:3-4 NLT).***

Likewise, Peter described that trials served a similar purpose as when heat is applied to unrefined gold, to purge it from the undesirable raw materials. Gold melts at a lower temperature than other elements, and will liquefy and separate from the dross, producing refined, purified gold. He said, ***"These trials will show that your faith is genuine. It is being tested as fire tests and purifies gold–though your faith is far more precious than mere gold. So when your faith remains strong through many trials, it will bring you much praise and glory and honor on the day when Jesus Christ is revealed to the whole world" (1 Peter 1:7 NLT).***

Consequently, the Lord "allows" assorted winds and storms of life, including sometimes even "allowing" Satan a "limited reach" *(Job 1:12, 2:6),* to bring troubles, trials, temptations to test our faith and spiritual character. This is so that such virtues of faith and persistence can rise to the challenge and emerge above the grip of the old fallen nature.

By "limited reach," we mean that God has restricted the extent and effect of such temptations and trials... and says that He will not allow us to be tested beyond what we are capable of. This doesn't mean that our trials will necessarily be a walk in the park. Some may be very severe. But it does mean that you will never face a trial that you do not have the ability to overcome.

This is very important to understand. You will never face any trial that you and Jesus cannot overcome. You see, when we became a follower of Christ, His Spirit and power was birthed within. And He wants each of us to learn how to yield to, and to exercise His power *(Ephesians 3:20)*... to rise in faith to conquer our challenges as well as to carry out works of ministry in His name.

The scripture says, ***"...God is faithful, who will not allow you to be tempted beyond what you are able, but with the temptation will also make the way of escape, that you may be able to bear it" (1 Corinthians 10:13).***

This promise of "escape" doesn't mean that we will necessarily evade all such troubles, but that He will enable us to "bear" them. In other words, through faith, our heart can "escape" into the sustaining presence and power of the Lord, which will enable us to "endure" such trying and difficult circumstances.

The Attitude of Faith

Finally, the great message of Romans 8:28 is intended to amplify optimism and to arouse an attitude of faith... to assure the Lord's followers that He loves us... and that despite whatever circumstances come our way, He will remain on our side, will never abandon us, and will always make everything work together for our good. After all, if He already gave the life of His own son for us, what else would He withhold from doing for you? *(Romans 8:31-32)*.

As with most things, attitude is everything and is more responsible for success or failure than anything else. As the well-known pastor Charles Swindoll once said, *"Words can never adequately convey the incredible impact of our attitudes toward life. The longer I live the more convinced I become that life is 10% what happens to us and 90% how we respond to it."*

So when troubles come our way, Romans 8:28 enables us to look at them without dread and pessimism, but with a new attitude of faith. You can have confidence that nothing can happen to us that God will not help us rise above... that He will ultimately turn around for good and use to our advantage. Trials need no longer to be a feared enemy, but an opportunity for our faith to be challenged and to grow.

To be sure, nothing can ever separate us from His parental love... and the Lord is aware of every incident in our life and loves us so very much that He will never allow us to face our difficulties alone or without purpose.

"Can anything ever separate us from Christ's love? Does it mean he no longer loves us if we have trouble or calamity, or are persecuted, or hungry, or destitute, or in danger, or threatened with death? ...I am convinced that nothing can ever separate us from God's love. Neither death nor life, neither angels nor demons, neither our fears for today nor our worries about tomorrow–not even the powers of hell can separate us from God's love. No power in the sky above or in the earth below–indeed, nothing in all creation will ever be able to separate us from the love of God that is revealed in Christ Jesus our Lord" (Romans 8:35,38,39 NLT).

Healing is One of God's Benefits

How to Receive Healing from God
Through Prayer and Faith

"Bless the Lord, O my soul, And forget not all His benefits: Who forgives all your iniquities, Who heals all your diseases." (Psalms 103:2-3)

The story is told of a young Irishman who once sought to purchase a boat fare to America, where he hoped to immigrate. From his years of savings, he discovered that he had sufficient to pay the fare, but not enough to pay for his meals aboard the ship. However, determined to seek the opportunity for a new life, he booked his passage and managed to scrape a few cents together for a meager bag of cheese and stale bread to carry him through his long journey.

One evening during the first two weeks at sea, the Captain was walking the deck when he noticed the Irishman sitting near the bow eating his cheese and bread.

"Why aren't you in the galley eating supper with the other passengers?" asked the Captain. The Irishman replied, *"I regret sir that I only had sufficient funds to buy passage, but not enough to pay for meals."*

The Captain looked at him curiously and said, *"Son, didn't you know that when you bought your ticket that your meals were included with your fare?"*

Just as the Irishman didn't realize that his meals were a benefit paid for in the price of his ticket, many Christians are unaware that Christ's atonement on the cross paid for other benefits besides eternal life. Just as the psalmist said in our text, **"Don't forget all the Lord's benefits! He forgives all your sins, and also heals all your diseases!"**

Healing is a Part of Christ's Atonement

Due to mankind's sin, which brought separation from God's fellowship, God sent Jesus to endure the sufferings and the brutal execution on the cross, "in our place," as our substitute, so that all mankind could have a "bridge" back to the fellowship and benefits of God. *"For He made Him who knew no sin to be sin for us, that we might become the righteousness of God in Him" (2 Cor. 5:21).*

Jesus not only purchased the salvation of our soul, but His sufferings also secured our physical healing. In fact, the word "salvation" so frequently used in the New Testament, comes from the Greek, *sōtēria (σωτηρία),* which means "wholeness and healing, both in the physical and spiritual."

Years before Jesus came to the earth, the prophet Isaiah described the sufferings of the Savior and their reason. He

wrote, ***"Surely He has borne our griefs and carried
our sorrows; yet we esteemed Him stricken, smitten
by God, and afflicted. But He was wounded for our
transgressions, He was bruised for our iniquities;
the chastisement for our peace was upon Him, and
by His stripes we are healed" (Isaiah 53:4-5).***

The stripes mentioned by Isaiah were the awful lashings
upon Jesus' back by the Roman whips. Thirty nine stripes
were the traditional punishment for a condemned
prisoner. According to the scripture, these stripes upon
Christ were in behalf of our healing *(1 Peter 2:24)*.

Is it God's Will to Heal?

Since the Bible indicates that healing is a part of the
reason of our Lord's sufferings, and is inseparable from
the idea of salvation, we must assume that it is as much
God's will to heal you as it is to save you! And of course we
know that the Lord wants everyone to be saved *(2 Peter
3:9)*.

Furthermore, the four Gospels show that during Jesus'
earthly ministry, there were eleven occasions that persons
approached Jesus for healing. Not once did Jesus turn
anyone away or state that it was not His will. This is
significant since the Bible is intended to show God's will
for man. In one instance, a leper came to Jesus inquiring
whether it was His will to heal him. He said, *"Lord, if it is*

your will, you can heal me." Jesus extended his hand and said, *"It's my will; Be healed!"* And the man's leprosy vanished *(Matthew 8:2-3).*

The scriptures confirm repeatedly that Jesus went about *"...healing all who were oppressed by the devil..."* *(Acts 10:38*). It also says, He went to the villages and towns... *"healing every sickness and every disease among the people." (Matthew 9:35).*

We know that from history, many people derived their names by what they did for a living. For instance, those named "Smith" came from generations of blacksmiths. It was a good way for a person to advertise their trade, "I'm Walter the Smith." Similarly, God identifies His own name by what He does. In the Old Testament, God says that His name is *Jehovah Rapha*, or *"I am the LORD that heals you" (Exodus 15:26).*

Think of it! God says that His name is **"The Lord that heals you!"** How could God reveal His will more clearly than to give himself a name that says He heals you? Not only is it His will, it's His name – it's who He is and what He does!

Five Steps to Receive Healing from God

(1) Submit yourself to God – As much as it is God's will and desire to heal, such things as unconfessed sin, disobedience, unbelief, or unforgiveness toward others can

hinder your reception of healing, and in some instances,
could actually be the original cause of your illness.

Any affliction should be a time for self-examination, to
come before the Lord in humility, surrendering yourself
and drawing near to Him. James wrote, ***"Therefore
submit to God. Resist the devil and he will flee from
you. Draw near to God and He will draw near to
you. Cleanse your hands, you sinners; and purify
your hearts, you double-minded. Lament and
mourn and weep! Let your laughter be turned to
mourning and your joy to gloom. Humble yourselves
in the sight of the Lord, and He will lift you up"
(James 4:7-10).***

(2) Look to God's Word – Read and meditate
continuously upon the healing promises in the Bible. As
you let them absorb into your inner man, it will bring a
great sense of assurance. This is the confidence of faith
that comes as you open your heart to the Word of God
(Romans 10:17). ***"My son, give attention to my words;
incline your ear to my sayings. Do not let them
depart from your eyes; keep them in the midst of
your heart; For they are life to those who find them,
and health to all their flesh" (Proverbs 4:20-22).***

How important it is that we focus upon God's Word, as
this is the source of His healing power. ***"He sent His
word and healed them, And delivered them from***

their destructions" (Psalms 107:20).

(3) Pray in Faith – Place your faith in the finished work of Christ's sufferings in behalf of your sickness or disease. Christ has already paid for your healing and has placed it into effect, making it available to you. Now it's up to you to accept His finished work by faith. *"Therefore I say to you, whatever things you ask when you pray, believe that you receive them, and you will have them" (Mark 11:24).*

(4) Call for Church Elders – Request for the elders or ministers of the church to anoint you with oil and pray the prayer of faith over you. The Bible says, *"Is anyone among you sick? Let him call for the elders of the church, and let them pray over him, anointing him with oil in the name of the Lord. And the prayer of faith will save the sick, and the Lord will raise him up. And if he has committed sins, he will be forgiven" (James 5:14-15).* Notice that it says the prayer of faith **SHALL SAVE THE SICK!**

Ask the elders and other believers to lay hands on you and pray. *"...they will lay hands on the sick, and they will recover" (Mark 16:18).* Again, notice that it says **THEY WILL RECOVER!**

(5) Keep Believing – Don't stop praying and believing! This is the most common reason why some people don't receive healing. They get discouraged and give up their faith. Most would prefer to have instantaneous healing, but most healings occur gradually over time.

Be patient and be steadfast in your faith. Keep praising and thanking Him for your answer. God will be faithful to His Word, if you will be faithful to believe! *"Do not become sluggish, but imitate those who through faith and patience inherit the promises" (Hebrews 6:12).*

— 12 —
Never the Same Again
The Legacy of My Mother's Prayers and the Story of How I Came to Jesus Christ

"Freeze! Don't move or I'll shoot!" The authoritative voice brought sudden fear and my heart pounded violently! As I turned toward the direction of the commanding words, I was shocked to find myself staring down the barrel of a .38 revolver! Just ten feet away, the plain-clothes detective pointed the gun nervously... the sun's reflection gleamed brightly from his chrome-plated badge.

The six of us, all teenagers, sat stunned and motionless along the creek, as the rustling sounds of police officers emerged from their hiding places in the dense woods. It was a drug bust. My pot-dealing friends and I had made the mistake to think we were secluded, but we were caught.

I was frightened and trembling. I had never been arrested before, nor had I ever had a gun pointed at my face. For a few moments, I became numb to the events around me, and my thoughts rambled through a surreal playback of past events in my life. For a moment I saw myself as a child sitting in Sunday School with a Bible in my lap. With tears swelling in my eyes, I heard the distant words, *"Oh how far away from God you have gone!"*

At the time of these things in 1971, I didn't realize that

this was the beginning of a number of life-shaking events that God would use to get my attention. Little did I know that my dear praying mother was on her knees day and night, seeking the Lord to bring her wayward son back to God.

Dale Robbins, Age 18

It's not as though I didn't know the right way. I was raised in a Christian home. From my earliest memories as a child in the Indiana farmlands, I could recall my parents taking their five children to church on Sundays. As a little boy, I can remember my lengthy prayers to God... and how Mother always reminded me that she had dedicated me to the Lord as a baby.

My life, however, took a different direction sometime during the seventh grade. I developed a fascination with drums, and started taking lessons. It wasn't long until I had become proficient enough to be promoted to the High School band. That same year I begged my parents for a drum set for Christmas, who, despite their modest means, did somehow produce a Sears and Roebuck set under the Christmas tree.

From that point, there were few days of peace and quiet around our house as I practiced and pounded day and night. Drumming became my niche in life. I advanced through the ranks of High School bands and orchestras, while after school I would join some of my guitar playing friends to practice top 40 rock and roll tunes.

When I was only fourteen, I received my first break into the world of music entertainment. A local professional group had recently lost their drummer, and with a schedule of dates to fill, they were searching frantically for a replacement. Someone suggested my name, and despite my young age (and my parent's objections), it wasn't long until I was traveling every weekend to night clubs and concert halls to perform with the reputed group. No longer did I have time for church. The Christian values I had grown up to believe, were rapidly becoming a faint memory, as I became more blinded by the bright lights of the world.

During the next six years, I climbed the ladder of rock and roll notoriety, playing with a number of popular hard rock groups... some who had performed with such greats as The Who, Sonny & Cher, REO Speedwagon, and many others who were well known in the late sixties and early seventies. However, in the rock music culture, I became exposed to a lot of new things I had not learned while growing up. Alcohol, drugs, immorality and every kind of perversion was commonplace in that environment. My parents never really knew the full extent of my involvements, only that I was far away from God.

One night, I was returning home in my fast new Chevy Camaro. I was rapidly approaching the crest of a hill at a high speed when the headlights of two vehicles suddenly appeared. Two late-night drag racers were speeding directly at me in both narrow lanes. There was no time to react, nor any place to go... the cars were only about 60 feet away.

The last thing I remember is thinking to myself, *"this is it! I'm going to die!"* as I let out a yelp and jerked the steering wheel hard to the right. Then came terrible sounds of screeching tires and grinding metal... the blur of headlights seemed to spin all around me, as smoke and dust billowed into the air.

For several minutes I was slumped over the steering wheel in a state of shock. When I gathered my composure, I looked up and could see the hazy image of dust still rolling in view of my headlights. I slowly pushed my door open and climbed out, but was trembling so violently I could barely stand up. Needless to say, I was amazed that I was still alive... and surprised to discover that I had no physical injury, or damage to my car. Neither was there any sign of the other two automobiles.

Looking at my car parked neatly in the side ditch, I wondered, *"did this really happen, or did I just hallucinate all this?"* But then I looked back at the road surface. Under the moonlight I could see the long black tire marks in every direction. The fresh odor of burnt rubber was in the air, and the residue of smoke and dust was still settling. No, it wasn't imaginary... but somehow my car passed by two others on a narrow strip of road without a scratch!

As I realized the impossibility of what just occurred, I collapsed onto the hood of my car and began to weep uncontrollably. I knew that God had something to do with saving my life. Once again, unbeknown to me, prayers were prevailing in my behalf. God had gotten my attention again, gradually bringing me to a place that I would consider His grace and mercy.

It was only a few weeks later that I began to experience an unusual series of personal disasters. I broke my hand in an accident, which effectively ending my drumming (for the time)... and I lost my day job, which was my primary means of support. I also suddenly became homeless. I had previously angrily, distanced myself from my family, who had challenged my sinful lifestyle.

Although it was the middle of one of the coldest winters on record, I had no place else to stay but in my car. At night, I parked on isolated country roads, and bundled myself in winter clothes to sleep. One night, the temperature became so cold (-20 degrees) that the back window of my car shattered and fell out. This brought me to a breaking point. I had lost everything that had been meaningful to me, and now I didn't even have any place to keep warm. Despair began to set in, and for many nights thereafter, I sat in my drafty car, stoned or drunk, contemplating ways to end my life.

One night, I was sifting through my belongings, and came across a box with a Bible inside. It was a keepsake that my sister gave me for my 13th birthday, but I had never read it. I began to cry as I looked through its pages. I remembered many of the stories about Jesus from Sunday School as a small child. For the first time in many years, I began to think about God. *"I wonder if God could change my life,"* I thought to myself.

Just a few days later, the lack of sleep and abuse of stimulants caught up with me. I passed out in a restaurant, and was taken to the hospital by ambulance. It was there that I saw my mother for the first time in many months. However, when I saw her, there was a difference about her. Though she had always been a professing Christian, she had recently been diagnosed with cancer, and had drawn closer to God than ever before. There was something new and vibrant about her. Her words were not condemning, but were kind... *"Dale, you need to let Jesus come into your heart and change your life."*

I was stunned by her statement. In all my years, I had

never heard my mother speak of Jesus in such a real and personal way. Though I didn't let on outwardly, her comments pierced my heart. I thought much about what she said... I also secretly spent more time reading in the Bible.

I was grateful that Mom welcomed me back home to live, and a few weeks later, shortly after my 20th birthday, she invited me to attend special services that were taking place at her church. I made up an excuse why I couldn't go, but inwardly I was curious about this church, and the change it had made in my mother's life. A couple weeks later, I drove by the church a few times to see if I could peek in and find out what it was like there. I could see nothing from the outside... but one night, I finally got up enough nerve to sneak in and sit on the back row after the service had started.

It had been a long time since I heard church hymns. Both the music and the simple sermon touched my heart deeply. Inside me, there was a melting, a stirring... tears trickled down my face during the whole service. Finally, the preacher said, *"If there's someone here tonight without God, I invite you to come to the altar and receive Jesus as your Lord and Savior."*

My heart began to pound. I knew something about altar calls from attending church as a kid. I knew it was where people prayed and made things right with God. I had mixed feelings. I wanted so much to reach out to God, but I also felt scared and wanted to run. Suddenly, I stood up to walk out the exit... but for some reason, instead of escaping, I turned and walked down the long aisle toward the altar.

Needless to say, my mother was stunned to see her son walking down the aisle that night. Finally at the altar, I collapsed to my knees, and there I wept as the pastor came and prayed with me, leading me in the sinner's prayer of repentance. For the next two hours, I continued crying at the altar, repenting of my sins and rebellion, surrendering my life to Christ. It was a moment that I would never forget... that changed my life forever.

For the first time in my life, God was no longer some ambiguous or distant entity. He was real, and His Spirit was now living in my Heart! When I walked from the church that night, there was a difference about me that I could not fully explain... I felt clean and different inside. Everything seemed new... even the moon and stars in the sky appeared brighter. From that night on, I never had a desire for drugs or alcohol again... I forsook a life of sin, and sincerely began to live as a Christian.

The reality of what Jesus did in my heart was so vivid that I had to tell others. I told my friends and family, and eventually took tracts and went out to the streets to witness and tell others about my discovery of the reality of

Jesus. It was never my intent to become a preacher or minister... something that was far from my thinking. But nearby churches asked me to share my story, and this eventually became my life's mission and passion, to share Jesus with others.

Many years have passed, but the reality of Jesus still remains as fresh and real today, as when He first came into my heart. **After I met Jesus, I was never the same again!** *(2 Corinthians 5:17)*

Jerri, Dale and Irene

Mom lived to see God answer her prayers, who brought her youngest son to Christ and called him into the ministry. This was her last photo with my wife Jerri and I. She passed away just months later.

CONCLUSION

I pray these articles and studies have been a blessing and encouragement to you, however before I conclude, I want to ask you one last question: **"Do you know for sure that you're saved, and that you would go to heaven should you die today?"**

I'm not asking whether you go to church, or if you believe that there is a God... but **"Do you know Jesus in a real and personal way? Have you received Him into your heart as your personal Savior and Lord?"**

If your answer is anything but an absolute YES, I ask you to make this the moment to remove all doubts, to put your faith in Jesus Christ, and accept the free gift of His salvation and eternal life that he offers you.

How to Become a Christian

It's so important to realize is that God loves you and wants to save you and have fellowship with you, but there's something that separates you from God... sin.

Sin is often thought of as some vile or immoral act, but the Bible helps us understand that it is much more... it is actually an attitude of rebellion against the ideals of God, intrinsic to our inherited human nature. In other words, it is the nature for all human beings to think, do or say things that violate God's holy standards.

According to scripture, this is a condition that was passed down to all the ancestors of Adam, the first man... who allowed sin to alienate himself from God's presence, and which continues to obstruct man's fellowship from the Lord today. The Bible says, ***"For all have sinned and fall short of the glory of God" (Romans 3:23).***

Not only does sin separate us from God in our present time, but it also maintains that separation beyond the grave... in a dreadful realm of eternal death and darkness that was never intended for mankind. The Bible says that the Lake of Fire was created as a place of everlasting punishment for the Devil and his angels, who sinned and rebelled against God, and were expelled from Heaven long ago.

Unfortunately, this hellish place will also be the shared destination of all those who remain separated from God when they face death. ***"And anyone not found written in the Book of Life was cast into the lake of fire" (Revelation 20:15).***

However, the great news is, rather than to abandon the fallen sinful human creatures that God originally created for His fellowship, God loved mankind so much that He devised a plan to redeem us, giving everyone an opportunity to make a choice... either to continue in sin and apart from God... or to turn to the Lord, receive His offer of forgiveness and walk in His fellowship. A relationship with the Lord brings new spiritual life and assurance of everlasting life with the Lord in Heaven when we die.

To implement His plan for redemption, however, God also had to find a way to comply with His own righteous standards by fulfilling His law of sin and death. In other words, according to God's values, death is an irrevocable consequence of sin that must be satisfied.... so in order to rescue man from death without violating His own principles, He found an alternate means to fulfill the demands of His law... by sending His son, Jesus, to die in our place. *"For the wages of sin is death, but the gift of God is eternal life in Christ Jesus our Lord" (Romans 6:23).*

The only sacrifice acceptable to fulfill this enormous debt in behalf of every man, woman and child on the earth, required a perfect, sinless sacrifice. Jesus, the son of God, was the only one who could take our place, since He is the only man without sin to ever walk on the earth.

So, God makes this amazing offer of forgiveness and salvation available as a free gift to every person, if they will comply with just one thing: To believe on the Lord Jesus Christ.

"For God so loved the world that He gave His only begotten Son, that whoever believes in Him should not perish but have everlasting life" (John 3:16).

To believe on Him means that by faith we accept that Jesus was indeed God's son, who came and died in our behalf on the cross, rose from the dead on the third day, and was exalted by the Heavenly Father as both our Savior and Lord.

The instant you acknowledge this reality in your heart and confess Jesus as your Lord and Savior, something extraordinary occurs... in fact, it is miraculous. The Spirit of Christ is born in your heart and you become a habitation of the Lord's presence. Becoming born-again brings new spiritual life, and God's promise of salvation and everlasting life. The Lord receives you as His child and He writes your name in the Lamb's Book of Life. ***"Rejoice because your names are written in heaven" (Luke 10:20).***

So are you ready to accept this gift of salvation that Jesus offers you right now? The scripture says, ***"If you confess with your mouth the Lord Jesus and believe in your heart that God has raised Him from the dead, you will be saved. For with the heart one believes unto righteousness, and with the mouth confession is made unto salvation" (Romans 10:9-10).***

Here's a sample prayer that you can put into your own words:

"Dear Lord Jesus, I realize that I am a sinner and that I need of your forgiveness. I believe that you died for my sins on the cross and rose from the dead so you could wash me of sin and give me eternal life. Please come into my heart now, forgive me and save me. I confess you as my Lord and Savior and place my faith in you. I will follow you as long as I live, and trust that when I die, you will receive me into Heaven. Thank you for your forgiveness, for coming into my heart, for making me a child of God!"

The very moment you sincerely express this prayer to Christ in faith, He will enter your heart by His Spirit. You may or may "not" feel or sense anything different at first... but don't be too concerned with that right now. For the moment, simply trust in His promise by faith. Jesus promised to save you, to forgive "all" your sins, and to write your name in His book of Life... at the very instant you call out for the Lord to come into your heart! And as you continue to walk in your new faith in Christ, you will begin to sense a growing awareness His inner peace, joy and presence along with other encouraging things in the days and weeks ahead.

After this, it's important to start reading the Bible each day to see what God has to say to you (start in the New Testament book of John)... and is equally important to talk to Him daily through prayer. Ask Him to guide your life and to fill you with the fullness His Holy Spirit.

Be sure to get involved with a good Bible-believing church and attend faithfully. Ask to be baptized in water at your earliest convenience, in obedience to what Lord commanded *(Acts 2:38)*, and by all means continue to live your life daily for the Lord!

If this book has inspired your life in Christ, please let us know. Please contact us at www.victorious.org.

www.ingramcontent.com/pod-product-compliance
Lightning Source LLC
Chambersburg PA
CBHW071832020426
42331CB00007B/1692